PERSPECTIVES THROUGH BLACK ICE

Burntside Speaks To Her People

by

Christine Moroni

PERSPECTIVES THROUGH BLACK ICE

Burntside Speaks To Her People

Written by *Christine Moroni*

Illustrations by *Helen Kuehlman*

Produced and Edited by
Charles Morello/IRIS Enterprises
Eveleth, MN

Published by
Singing River Publications
P.O. Box 72
Ely, MN 55731

ISBN 0-9709575-1-3

Printed by
Davidson Printing Company
Duluth, MN

Perspectives
Through
Black Ice

Burntside Speaks To Her People

Reflections
on the seasons of the year
in the seasons of the heart

by

Christine Moroni

Dedication

*To the Great Spirit who resides
in the black ice and changing
seasons of my heart.*

Introduction

This publication initiates a new beginning for me in creative endeavor. Thankfulness is my theme. First, I am grateful to nature, the gift of God, which has inspired me and sustained my life these many years. I am thankful for family, friends, and the community for supporting and encouraging this work. To Helen Kuehlman, many thanks for the sensitive and representative watercolor art and sketches. Chuck and Carol Morello of *IRIS Enterprises* deserve a special thanks for superb technical, editing, and publishing assistance. Thank you also to G. W. Tucker, photographer, who transcribed Helen's watercolors for publication.

My hope for all who read this prose is that they will be renewed and energized by observing and participating in the perspectives of the seasons of the northland. Do read it in the early morning light of sunrise or by the light of evening twilight as a reminder of the beauty and experience of nature.

Christine Moroni
June, 2001

Table of Contents

BLACK ICE

Black ice is a season and a state of mind. It bridges the gap between eternal summer and deepest winter.

There's a rhythm to this black ice season. It ebbs and flows with late autumn, winter, and early spring, but it does not belong exclusively to any season.

It was four below zero at daybreak. That's not unusual in the Boundary Waters Canoe Area Wilderness (BWCAW), but it is a little rare in the middle of November.

I watched the steam rise off the lake. Although the lake temperature was about 35 degrees, it was a sight warmer than the air temperature. The steam crystallized on the Norway pine needles, flocking them with decoration which could never be duplicated in any Christmas shop.

Hoist Bay on Burntside Lake was transformed into a fairyland scene. The rising sun's rays caught the flocked shoreline and rebounded off the lake. In the shallows, a layer of ice formed so thin it flexed with the gentle rolling movement of the lake.

Some of the hoar frost was blown off the trees onto the

shoreline ice. A frosting of snow decorated shoreline reeds and rushes.

The rebounding sun's rays boomeranged from shoreline ice to the aquamarine of open water. The morning gleamed.

Later, the wind picked up. At minus four degrees, it was biting and raw on exposed skin. Water splashed on shoreline rocks and froze to the granite surface in seconds. The morning still gleamed.

November sun, a rarity in northern Minnesota, turned the aquamarine lake a deep blue. Occasional blaze-orange-clad deer hunters used boats and motors to cross the thickening water to favorite stands on the northwest shore of the lake. This was their last chance until next year.

The afternoon still gleamed and the lake assumed a patient waiting stance. Gradually the day began to cool. The sun had crossed the sky and stayed low on the horizon. The wind dropped and the lake got quiet. A motor boat returned three hunters from the northwest side of the lake. The sunset was yellow, purple, and gray.

The blue of the lake deepened, first to purple and then, as the sun set, to black. Dark transformed the landscape to angular shadows and hues of gray.

Night's blackness was upon the land early, and I heard, imperceptibly at first, the delicate squeaking of ice formation as crystals bonded for the first time. I compared the rhythm of the day to the season and rhythm of my heart.

* * *

For weeks now, the sun had been low in the sky behind the hill. It was mid-December. The lake was booming. Freeze-up was in its final stages. It was possible to walk on the ice near the shore.

I anticipated the days ahead. Soon I could skate. Maybe I could go for a mile or more down the shore if heavy snow didn't arrive too early.

Then it was time. I scraped the snowy surface, and the ebony ice glowed back at me. Shadows of birch and balsam stretched and grew long in the sunny January afternoon. I skated, and I was flying. I scraped again and gained a philosophy and wisdom deeper than I had known.

Evening came early. I skated on. A Laplander fire burned near the frozen shore. It glowed deeply into the winter night. Time stood still. The rhythm of the day, of the season, and of me, were one.

By February, the black ice of Burntside Lake is 24 to 36 inches thick and is covered with knee-deep snow. Now, both the ice and I cover a thrumming, silent but living current deep within us. In good time the wellspring of strength and ideas will break forth in yet another rhythm of another season.

* * *

Slush forms on black ice. The spring song of the chickadee is strong and daily. Shadows are still too long for a spring state-of-mind. On the east sides of islands, dark spots begin to appear around shoreline rocks and fallen logs. Still, the ice is black.

Then one day, the evergreens begin to lose their blue-black aura. The spring sun is higher in the sky. The ice begins to honey-comb. The west-southwest wind blows in undulating waves. Under the ice, the black water responds to the call of the wind to be free. The human heart does the same.

This rhythm of freedom is strong. It becomes a state-of-being for every living thing. The time for the darkness of introspection is over. The lake breaks free of its icy bond and reflects the blue of the sky instead of the blackness of its own interior. The human heart does the same.

MIDNIGHT SKI – MOONLIGHT SKI

It was minus twelve degrees Fahrenheit on the porch thermometer. I stepped outside and onto the porch where split and dried wood was stacked. All was still. No wind. The moon was half in a cloudless night sky.

As if by magic I was beckoned to ski. I went back inside and dressed for a cold ski – three layers top and bottom, wool cap, face mask, and "hot fingers" ski gloves.

I waxed my skis with polar – the wax for below-zero temps. First I crayoned the entire ski and corked it smooth. Then I slapped on a kick wax over the foot area. Perfect.

The snow squeaked as I pushed off and poled around the cabin to my ski trail. It was cold all right, but the wax was perfect. There was no need for a headlamp. The moon was brilliant against the snow. Its light caused fresh snow crystals to gleam like diamonds. It was exciting to be alive.

The trail took me in a round-about fashion down to the lake. As I shot down the rill and onto Burntside ice, I felt thrilled and privileged to be a part of this beauty. The lake was a sheet of snow and diamonds. Orion hunted bravely in the southwest sky. The big ipper hung low and upside down, dumping its contents into the lake. And Draco the Dragon prowled his territory, helped by the light of the moon.

Eastward across the lake I steamed, clouds of breath rising just ahead of my line of vision. The face mask frosted. So did the front of my jacket. Even the moon took on a flourescent glow when frosted breath interfered with my line of vision.

Past Hoist Bay, past Outlet Bay, and eastward toward Sig Olson's Listening Point. Nothing stirred. All was dark.

I swung south and then west, backtracking until I skied even with the public landing. A snowmobile trail ribboned onto the lake from the landing. Just the thing.

The shore and woods offered their own kind of beauty. Mooncast shadows of balsam and naked birch and poplar criss-crossed the trail. I skied on my shadow, ski-tips just passing my head with each stride.

Although the temperature continued to fall, I was toasty. The skis floated on the fresh trail snow. I drank deeply from the intoxicating cup of midnight winter magic.

It was a timeless exhilarating moment.

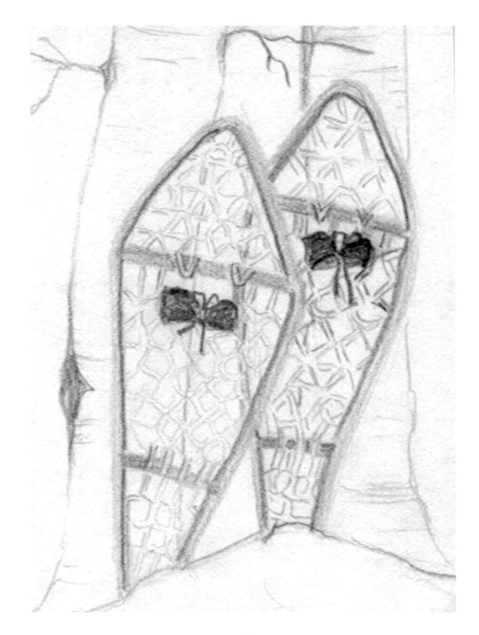

JANUARY THAW

A Respite From Winter's Grip

It was a Saturday in mid-January. The snow was in seven and eight foot piles outside the window. A two-day blizzard had just dumped a fresh twenty inches of snow onto an already white world. Birch trees gleamed in the snow and sunshine.

The sky was a cloudless bright blue, and the temperature was about 30 degrees Fahrenheit. Wearing a pair of corduroys, a chamois shirt, and wool socks, I stepped out of doors onto the porch, and braced myself for a wintry blast of wind. It didn't happen. What's this? The air was soft; the wind gentle.

Back inside I went for my Sorrels. I walked outside again, down the porch steps, and around to the south side of the cabin. The January noonday sun hit me full force. It was glorious. Every body pore soaked up the sun's warmth. At the feeder, chickadees chirped their approval of the respite from thirty below winter conditions.

What a day to be outside! On a day like this there are many activities to consider. I could snowshoe a new path to the lake and

break a trail down the shoreline. I could re-break my ski trail down the logging road. That would be fun, especially because I could wear sweats and wind pants instead of heavy wool. I could skate on the black ice rink of Burntside Lake. I might even get a sunburn! And at the same time, I could ice fish if I took the time to re-drill a hole not fifty feet from the rink. I could walk the road and immerse myself in the quiet of this winter day in the woods. And while I walked, I would dream of other woods things – like picking strawberries in the spring, canoeing my favorite lake in the BWCAW, building a sauna, splitting wood, sanding my canoe paddle – the list is always endless.

My thoughts were interrupted by the throaty gurgle of a raven. It had spotted some bread which I'd put out on a stump. The gray jays and chickadees had seen it too. My silent reverie changed to one of entertainment. Each species had its own method of feeding, standing guard for each other, and protecting the cache.

The chickadees darted and swooped and landed right on the heel of a loaf of bread. They would eat a few mouthfuls quickly and then get out of the way for the next black cap.

The routine was interrupted only when a bigger bird came in to feed. The whiskey jack did just that. His gray tuxedo was smooth until he landed. Then the feathery creature ruffed his coat, grew to enormous proportions in a matter of seconds, and frightened the chickadees away.

The jay's banquet was short-lived, however. The ravens were back. Size-wise the grays didn't have a chance. Those black, three-foot raven wing spans were just too much. The greedy birds helped themselves liberally to the bread.

The longer that I remained outside, the more I noticed little things. There was the wrinkled, red, rose hip nodding in the early afternoon breeze. How had it survived thus far?

The red flower buds on the maple tree were beautiful in this whiteness. I was reminded that the promise of spring *was* legitimate – even with eight or ten weeks of hard weather ahead.

In the spring, tree flowers do not catch the interest of the average observer. They're too subtle. But today they were virtually shouting their beauty to the silent land. And I was listening.

Shadows were cast on the snow by dogwood, alder, and poplar brush. In another season, these growths would not encourage beauty in the eye of the beholder. They would be browse for deer and rabbit.

They would impede the path of man as hunter or nature lover. But today, their patterns resembled crocheted lace on the snowy land. Additional shadows displayed by balsam and spruce seedlings contributed even more delicacy to an already flawless visual piece.

I noticed a change in myself. My spirits were high. Surge after surge of joyous thought washed over me like cleansing surf. Childhood memories of winter fun, present contentment with the beauty of the day, and future dreams crystallized in a mental video of appreciation.

Spring fever – cabin fever. First attack of the year. I laced up my boots, put on my jacket and cap, and started down the road. After supper tonight, maybe, just maybe, I'd begin to sand my canoe paddle.

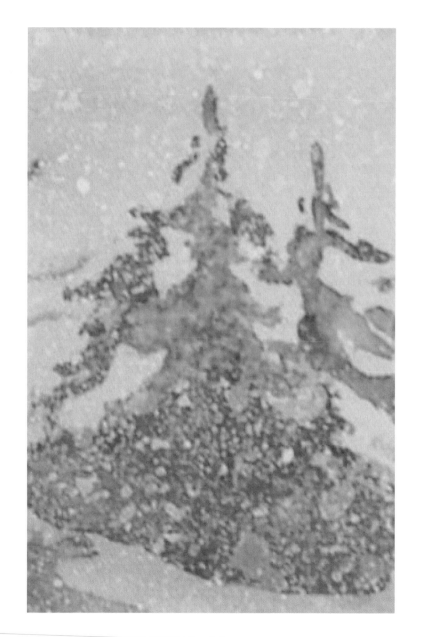

SPRING MOON

There it was, just over the purple tips of the birches – the moon, almost full. It did my heart good to see it. The day had been warm but gray. Toward late afternoon, the sun had broken through the clouds and made the camp supper a time to remember. Soup, cheese, crackers, and hot tea never tasted so good. More than that, though, was the sense of belonging to the woods.

There was a sense of peace and an appreciation of the white stillness. To be sure, there was also a keen realization to which I was grounded. The realism was that it was late winter in the BWCAW. Nature plays no favorites. This was a time to keep woods knowledge and common sense foremost in my mind – for survival.

It was mid-March in the BWCAW. I was on quarter break and the week was my own. There was plenty of snow in the woods.

For these two days I was tucked into a snow cave on Glimmer Lake on a little-used campsite. The door of the cave faced southwest and I was out of the wind. It was exciting in an odd sort of way – cozy and fun, too.

Perhaps that is why, despite the seriousness of the snowy

conditions, the evening was especially beautiful. The temperature allowed for an "evening program" before tucking into the mummy bag. This program consisted of a short ski across the portage and onto the lake.

I shot onto the white expanse and drew a deep breath. Pristine. Was it my imagination or did I really smell balsam fragrance in the moist night air? Another deep breath. Unspeakably beautiful. Moonlight reflected off the snow made the lake and forest as bright as day.

The moonlight cast balsam and birch shadows onto the lake. I wished for a friend with whom to share this time. But skiing is a silent business. What mattered was that I was experiencing this gift of timeless, age-old beauty.

From where I stood, I could see the glow of the campfire in the campsite grate. It looked homey and inviting. Another fifteen minutes and I'd be ready to respond to the warmth of the fire and the sleeping bag.

This was a far cry from my cedar log cabin where icicles hung from the roof and reflected moonlight like a hundred tiny prisms. It was the moonlight on the icicles that compelled me to camp. Even more than the cabin scene, I wanted to be "out in it."

And out in it I was. The mild winter weather felt good.

Every sense was alive. The only sound was a gentle night wind through the black-green pines. The moonlit lake was a sight to behold. The smell of wet earth and moss was hanging in the moist air.

The whole experience was to my taste – even more than the

hot chocolate and brandy that were waiting for me in camp. A sigh of contentment escaped me.

In the deep of winter, a spring moon stirred hope and anticipation of the coming summer. Though the reality of seasons teaches otherwise, eternal summer reigns in our hearts, in our dreams, and in our waking moments. We long for it; we pine for it. The thought of it sustains us through difficult times.

Spring moon is the herald of those dreams. It bridges the expanse between deep winter and eternal summer.

In the deep of winter, a spring moon marks the time and bestows a beauty all its own. Smiling, I broke my reverie and double-poled back to camp.

The winter sky glowed with stars and snow-reflected moonlight. Night was day, or so it seemed. And it went on and on until the first light of dawn gave a new challenge to the stars in the sky.

FIRST TRIP UP

Early April is about the time that I start thinking about summer canoe trips and fishing. There is always a time (sometimes just a day) when the earliness of summer is first realized by my winter-weary brain. It is the moment *before* the tree buds swell, *before* the ground is soft, *before* the snow is completely gone. And so it was this April. The excitement of springtime upon me and the anticipation of being in the woods urged me into action. The action was, of course, taking that first canoe paddle up the St. Louis River for a weekend.

My friend Jean owns a hunting cabin (she calls it a shack) in the wilds of the St. Louis River area. She was ready and happy to make the trip too, right down to bringing a carton of fresh strawberries for the celebration of spring. We packed the night before and left for the river right after school on Friday afternoon. Although it was late April, and fishing season was not open, I purchased a license when we stopped for gas. This further heightened my expectations for the coming summer and gladdened my heart.

My spirits lifted again as we passed the abandoned railroad

section house and bumped down three miles of old railroad bed to Skibo Mill landing. It was late afternoon. By this time the 70 degree warmth of the day had dissipated and there was a cool southeast wind blowing. I put on a sweatshirt over two other layers of cotton clothing. I was looking forward to a quiet paddle up the river, a warm fire, and freshly baked pizza for supper. This would be topped off with fresh strawberries and hot tea laced with brandy.

As we rounded the first bend in the river, we saw smoke moving across the sky from the southeast. Fire. But where? Conversation is not essential while paddling a canoe. We noted the smoke and watched it. We didn't speculate aloud on various possibilities.

By the time we had paddled three hundred yards it was evident that this fire was close to that area around Jean's shack. Soon U. S. Forest Service planes were flying into the smoke. This was followed by a helicopter laden with firefighting equipment. It was going to be a noisy weekend at best. Maybe we'd be serving coffee and sandwiches to the fire fighters. We kept paddling.

It soon became apparent that the fire was located directly in the area of Jean's shack. As we paddled closer we could see thick billowing clouds of smoke and then flames which torched the dry spruce and exploded them into fireballs in a matter of seconds. We felt the heat. The river was full of ash. The fire, whipped by the southeast wind, swept down the shoreline, jumped the river, and continued its rampage into the forest not fifty yards from the cabin.

In silence we paddled through the smoke until we were up stream of the burning. Then we sat and watched and listened to the sound of that fire. There was nothing else to do. We waited until the sound of the fire had lessened. We watched as bigger planes dropped tons of water and flame retardant on the fire which was spreading to the northwest. And we floated back downstream watching the fire cut directly through Jean's lot.

After a time it got quieter. The woods were still burning on both sides of the river. But where we were, the big trees had already burned and the burning brush didn't look as terrible as the holocaust of white pine and spruce trees "going up." Things seemed to be slowing down.

Jean wanted to go into the woods to see what the situation was with her cabin. We pulled the canoe up on shore where the fire had not burned and loosely tied it to a bush. Following a cross-country ski trail which had been cut and used the winter before, we arrived at the cabin clearing. What a surprise. The woodpile was standing, the shack was totally intact, and the outhouse was burned to the ground. All that remained of it was a charred hole.

Jean unlocked her cabin door, ran into the house, and grabbed her radio, three sleeping bags, and her father's fishing rod. The fire was still burning in and around the whole area so we didn't spend much time standing around. We did stomp out a small blaze directly in front of the porch. What a helpless feeling.

With booty in hand we ran back to the canoe. Fire was still moving down the shoreline. We had to move out. It took us about an hour to reach the landing. We loaded equipment back into the truck and returned to town exhausted.

II

Thirty-six hours later we were headed once again for the St. Louis River and Jean's shack. Keeping our thoughts and expectations to ourselves, we shoved off.

There was smoke in the sky but not in concentrated billows as it was on Friday evening. The helicopter was "chopping" its way in and around the smokey forest. The fire was definitely burning, but the center of it seemed scattered – not as intense.

When we arrived at the shack's canoe landing, four forest rangers (fire fighters) in yellow hard hats greeted us. They had been flown in from the state of Michigan. Fire fighting equipment was strewn all over the landing. It was gratifying to see gas water pumps connected to hoses which ran and forked through the woods.

"Is it still there?" Jean asked one of, the guys.

"Yep, it is," was the reply. So we landed the canoe and quietly walked the 100 feet from the river to the cabin site.

It was a sight to behold. There it stood amid the ash and burned tree trunks. A miracle. The woods were still smoking around us. We proceeded to have a picnic. No roasted hot dogs, you understand. Just bologna sandwiches, an orange, cookies, and water. We sat in the shade of the cabin and continued to be amazed by the sights around us.

The fire crew was about twenty strong in the river area. There were four fire fighters on the landing and the rest were located at various points along the river and inland. One stopped to talk briefly. He gave instructions kindly. Stay near the cabin. Do not venture into the fire areas. Rake debris and dead leaves away from the cabin foundation.

We asked about the origin of the fire. Lightning? Sparks from a train? A tossed cigarette butt?

"No," said he. "This was a prescribed burn that got out of hand." Why the U. S. Forest Service would conduct an intentional burn in a tinder-dry forest with 30 mile per hour winds was beyond our understanding. He assured Jean that the government would compensate her for the destroyed outhouse.

As we were eating lunch, a "hot spot" near the picnic site burst into flames. It happened not 20 feet from us. We grabbed buckets of water and doused the blaze. For the rest of the afternoon we stayed near the cabin and doused "hot spots."

By evening we were fatigued. The fire burned on further up the river, but still close enough to see. It was time to leave again. This time though, there was a different feeling. The cabin was standing; a fire crew stood ready. Our emotions centered on hope and comfort. The forest would eventually renew itself. And there would be other times to anticipate spring with strawberries and tea laced with brandy.

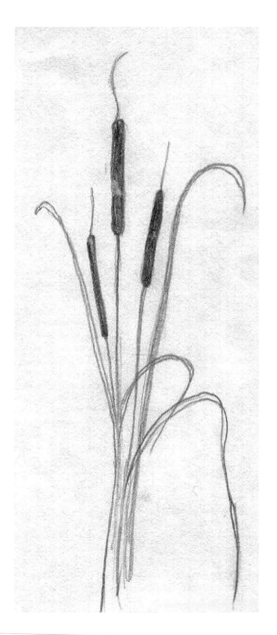

A LOON STORY

Actually, it happened quite by accident. There we were on a Monday afternoon getting blown about on Thomas Lake. We were fishing the shoreline for northern pike, and the fishing was poor. Temp was about 48 degrees Fahrenheit, June 13th. Miserable weather. As we were batted about in the canoe by the wind, Rosie saw her. She was so still it was difficult to know if our eyes were playing tricks on us. There, at the base of a rocky precipice facing southwest, was a loon sitting on her nest. Her head and neck were down flat against the edge of the nest and inches from the water. She blended perfectly with the granite background.

When we finally determined that this was in fact a loon, we thought she might be dead. But no – that black head and beady red eye watched every move of our canoe being tossed about by wave action. It seemed that she picked a nesting spot which was not only out of the way, but conveniently warmed by the sun's direct rays and which also reflected and refracted rays from the rocky ledge behind the nest.

She stayed put on the nest and we moved away as

non-chalantly as possible. But inside we were excited. Would it be possible to photograph her without causing a ruckus?

Rosie had a telescopic wide-angle lens on her camera, which made the whole idea possible. She considered the problem, the various angles, the light and exposure problems.

The next day we decided to give the photography a try. Weather was none too cooperative. It continued to blow and mist and we wondered whether the situation warranted us even trying. But, we paddled into the bay and drifted as quietly as possible toward the nest. Click, click, went the camera.

She was off the nest in a flash, churning the water with her wings. Her mate appeared out of nowhere and hooted once quietly as if to tell his mate that he was there and supported her. He began to draw us away from the nest. We followed with Rosie snapping shutters as fast as she could focus. Not a sound was uttered, either by the loon pair or us. As we paddled away, she was once more ensconced on her nest, warming two brown eggs.

FRONT COMING IN

The first sign of a storm front coming in is the noticeable increase in insect activity. Moths cling to the log walls of the cabin. Black flies become pests. They nip at naked ankles, knees, and elbows. They congregate on screens and do not leave. If they are shooed, they return promptly. Picnic food is infested with curious and hungry deer flies. It becomes almost impossible for a human being to sit outside undisturbed.

This predictable behavior should be a signal to us. If we are aware of it, we begin to look for other signs which confirm our suspicion of weather change.

The air feels heavy and full of moisture. There is no breeze. The lake is calm – just a hint of current moves it. Although the sun is shining, the sky is hazy. The leaves of trees and undergrowth hang heavy – as though the weight of the atmosphere is too much for their slender stems.

"Ah-ha," we say, "front coming in." And as the afternoon progresses, changes, imperceptible at first, then bolder, take place.

The sky begins to "cloud-up." Billows of cumulonimbus clouds form in the southwest and begin to move in a northeast direction across the sky. The wind is a soft breeze. The trees respond gratefully to the movement of the wind and rustle and nod in the humid afternoon. The lake has infinite ripples looking much like a road full of "washboard bumps." The flies are frantic in their efforts to combat the stillness.

Now is a good time to take a swim. The lake is a refreshing change from the sticky, humid, fly-infested air. No wonder the deer head for the water during fly season.

Slowly, slowly, the thunderheads rumble in. They are purple-black and cover the whole southwestern sky. There is thunder, but only faint. This is the time to "batten down the hatches, "to put lawn chairs inside, to cover the woodpile.

Then it is here – this front (or is it *an affront*?). The wind begins a steady movement through the birches. They nod in appreciation, in acceptance, and begin their dance. They bend and toss and bend again, much like maidens in a dance with their beloved.

Rain begins in mist. Tiny drops of water make a haze as the dusty road becomes damp. The wind, ever present and invisible, pushes the storm clouds directly overhead. The lake begins to roll. Thunder roars. The heavens open, and a steady, pelting, penetrating rain soaks the forest. The smell of damp earth and wet leaves is everywhere. Lightning flashes, followed immediately by an explosion of thunder. The storm is directly overhead. I listen to the thrashing and feel relief from the heavy, humid air and from the buzzing flies (now disappeared). The lake has whitecaps now. The rolls have turned into waves. They race down the lake with and ahead of the storm.

But this is not an electric storm. This is a hard rain. It's cozy on the porch, watching. Even though the air temperature has gone down about ten degrees, it is warm. And I'm out of the wind.

After a while the wind stops blowing. All that I can hear is the steady 'shush' of raindrops on birch leaves. It continues uninterrupted until every thirsty thing is satisfied. The trees are still. The lake reflects the gray-purple sky, but has ceased its endless roll. The air is fresh and the humidity has lifted.

Later still, there is a quieting as the rain gradually ceases. Water dripping from birch leaves onto raspberry bushes makes a plopping sound. Soon even this is still.

This symphony of sound quiets to pianissimo. Not a tree stirs – not a leaf. The lake is a giant, silver mill pond. And all of nature holds its breath to catch the final note of this composition, this melody, which can be heard only in the stillness – the last percussive

flourish of water on leaf.

PICKING WILD STRAWBERRIES

Wild strawberries are a delicacy, albeit hard-earned. The fruit is tiny compared with the luscious golf-ball-sized fruit of the commercial pickeries. However, wild berries are pungent and hold a fierce wild flavor that is unmistakably north woods in identification.

As I said, picking wild strawberries is hard work, even back-breaking work. Finding a patch worth picking takes considerable luck and planning. This means surveying a large area of land in early spring just to see where the strawberry plants lie. The effort has to be made before other foliage greens up. The white flowers that precede the berry are highly visible to the naked eye. These flowers come along about the middle part of May and make eyeballing the length and breadth of the patch quite easy. Good strawberry patches are found along railroad tracks, on sandy hillsides, along logging roads, and on old railroad beds where tracks and ties have been removed.

The actual picking time runs from about June 15, in an early season, until just past the Fourth of July. All of a sudden, one day, little red jewels are there hiding under grassy undergrowth and camouflaged by the red strawberry leaves themselves. It is exciting

to see these first berry fruits of the season. I marvel at the short gestation from winter's last blast (usually in April) to the finished product of mid June. Year after year, I am never disappointed.

Oh yes – the difficulties involved in picking are worth mentioning. First of all, there is the back strain of it. The plants and fruit are about two or three inches from the ground.

This means stooping, bending, sitting, or crawling around on hands and knees for a cup or two of berries. In the process, we encounter other challenges.

The number two challenge is the insect world of mosquitoes, black flies, and wood ticks. These creatures stage an all-out attack on intruders who would have a few strawberries. The invasion of their territory is no friendly matter. Mosquitoes hum loudly and attack every visible body orifice. Black flies are more subtle. They sneak up silently and make straight for the hair line, sock line, collar, or shirt cuff. They are known, much like inconsiderate golfers, for not "replacing the turf." The wood ticks are the most silent of all. They attach themselves to skin or clothing and then quietly seek their spot. This might be an arm pit, an ear, or the back of a knee.

Stained pants or socks are the number three challenge. Clothing will never be the same. Socks will forever bear the red badge of courage (turned brown) of the strawberry patch.

Other incidental challenges are the heat of a mid-day June sun and wet "ishy" places into which one inadvertently steps or kneels.

"Then why do it at all?" you ask. Yes indeed, why? Commercial berries are so readily available. The answer to this question lies in the personal philosophic vein.

There is something about getting out. during the days before, during, and after spring solstice. There is a beauty in a five a.m. sunrise that will hold me through many days of winter darkness. There is a morning freshness that makes me want to stand still in the moment, holding the thrilling, piercing energy of morning beauty. There is the plunge into Burntside Lake when the picking is over; the water washing through my hair and ringing in my ears. There is the evening pick – with misty coolness rising from the roadside ferns before sunset. The dusty-misty haze glows in the evening light and turns color as the sun's rays reflect off hill and lowland.

Once in a lifetime there is a special memory. It can happen without fanfare or warning. It can be prophetic. It can be magic. All that is required is to be out there – picking wild strawberries.

For me the moment came late on a June evening. I was walking the road in half sunlight, half twilight. The strawberries were there, but I had seen better years and bigger fruit.

I knelt to pick a small patch of about twenty-five plants. Suddenly, there was a snapping of twigs and a crashing of underbrush in the swamp. A bear? I crouched low in the grass and waited. In less than half a minute, a fawn, spots on its back, burst out of the swamp and up the road embankment running at full tilt.

It ran right at me, ignored me, and raced past me with white tail up, never breaking stride. Its hoofs clattered on the loose gravel of the road, and in a moment it was over the hill.

Momma deer was nowhere to be seen. The forest was silent.

Even the pesky crows had shut up. What was going on? I didn't have long to wonder. There was more crashing through the underbrush. I stayed crouched in the tall roadside grass and watched a gray-black wolf with tawny hind quarters slug through the wetness of swamp grass and fallen logs. He was hot on the trail of the fawn.

When the wolf was about twenty feet from me, I stood up. It slowed, stopped, and looked at me. Immediately it turned and moved quickly back the way it had come, glancing furtively over its shoulder and disappearing around a copse.

I stood in the road, mentally and emotionally absorbing the action of the past few minutes. The woods were silent. It was as if the whole forest knew what had happened and no one was telling!

Suddenly a white-throated sparrow sang its familiar tune, "Oh Can-a-da, Can-a-da!" The starkness of fear was broken. Once again the rhythmic energy of the evening took hold. The woods began to hum.

It was time to go home. My shoes crunched on the gravel. My mind and heart wondered and reflected on what I had been privileged to witness. I felt a part of the woods, a part of nature.

It happened without warning, without fanfare. All that was required was to be out there – picking wild strawberries.

A FISHING BAGATELLE

"If you have never caught a stream trout in a lake, you haven't lived," says Michael Furtman in his book, *A Boundary Waters Fishing Guide*. It's true. The experience for me was exhilarating, challenging, bittersweet, and just plain fun.

During the middle of June, four women made a Boundary Waters Canoe Area Wilderness circle canoe trip beginning at Little Indian Sioux entry point on the Echo Trail north of Ely, Minnesota. The group included Rose Schleif (physical education instructor at Mt. Scenario College), Ann Pesavento (music instructor at Gustavus Adolphus College), Jean McCurdy (physical education instructor at Mesabi Community College), and I, Chris Moroni (music instructor at Mesabi Community College).

Besides being an opportunity to "get away from it all,' this was also a fishing trip. The lakes along the Canadian Border always hold promise of fishing success in the spring of the year. We hoped for the best.

We got our BWCAW permit and drove for about an hour up the Echo Trail. A game warden was waiting to check the permit and

canoe stickers. All was in order.

We took off down the first portage trail to the river. Then it was into Upper Pauness and across the portage around Devil's Cascade.

The lakes and campsites were in good condition. Not many canoe parties venture this far north from the Echo Trail in "paddle only" waters. The water was clean and cold. Usually, June waters are too cold for swimming. This time, the steady 90 degree Fahrenheit temperatures had warmed the lakes so that swimming was not only a possibility, but a good idea.

Mosquitoes and black flies were almost non-existent. The hot, dry weather had thwarted their breeding and hatching season. Woodticks, however, were thick in the high, dry, jackpine country. When we camped on a point in East Loon Bay, they almost picked up the tent and carried it off!

We had one visitor – unannounced. A large snapping turtle was attracted to our three freshly-caught bass. She made a meal of our shore lunch and encouraged us to swim elsewhere for that afternoon.

For two full days we paddled and portaged until Lac La Croix lay before us. Beautiful! It was time to set up camp and stay a while.

After the camp chores had been done, we decided to fish one of the small adjoining lakes. We took our supper with us (soup, cheese, and crackers), and headed out using two canoes.

Excitement rose high as we reached the trout lake. What could we expect this evening? We began to troll the lakeshore slowly. There was one hit almost immediately, but nothing more. We changed lures. Still nothing. Then we thought we'd still-fish and/or cast. This went on for an hour. Not a bite; not a sign of life.

I finally got hungry enough to request transportation to shore to fix supper. Ann and Jean had taken one canoe and gone sightseeing, but had just returned. The fire was going.

Rosie was fishing alone just off the campsite. Suddenly a rainbow trout hit her lure. There was thrashing and some shouting. But, the fish threw the bait and was gone. What a disappointment!

Rosie said, "Enough. I'm ready for soup and cheese."

As we ate, we watched the sun turn the clouds pink. The sky was reflected in the lake. There wasn't a ripple or a breath of movement.

It was time to head back to the camp, but Rosie wasn't ready to give up. 'How about ten casts each?" she said. I said, "Okay," In a minute we were in the canoe leaving Jean and Ann to clean up the supper dishes.

By this time the water was dark. we put on small spoons and began to cast. On my third cast, a streak of silver exploded into the air. A two-and-a-half pound rainbow trout had hit the line and was on! What a fighter! He put a small mouth bass to shame.

Oh-oh. Trouble. The monofilament line twisted around the line guide on the fishing rod. Rosie helped me get it off and was waiting with the landing net. What a beautiful fish! The pink rainbow stripe was quite a contrast to its silver sides.

But wait! Another rainbow had hit. This time it was Rosie's line. Another fighter! I waited with the net. Another beauty on the stringer and thoughts of trout for breakfast.

Now it really was time to go. We had little daylight left to navigate the lake and portage. First we took some photos (bragging pictures) and headed back.

The fish were gutted but were on the stringer, attached through the heads. We paddled back, still excited. Ann and Jean had gone on ahead. All of a sudden tragedy struck. As we paddled into the camp area, the fish heads on the stringer snapped. Four pounds of rainbow trout breakfast sank in 20 feet of water. It was totally dark. The fish were irretrievable. An expletive cut the air. Then silence. There was nothing to say.

We beached the canoe and quietly came into the camp. Fatigue and mosquitoes were too much for us. The sleeping bags were inviting. So, we called it a day and fell asleep, dreaming of those magnificent rainbows.

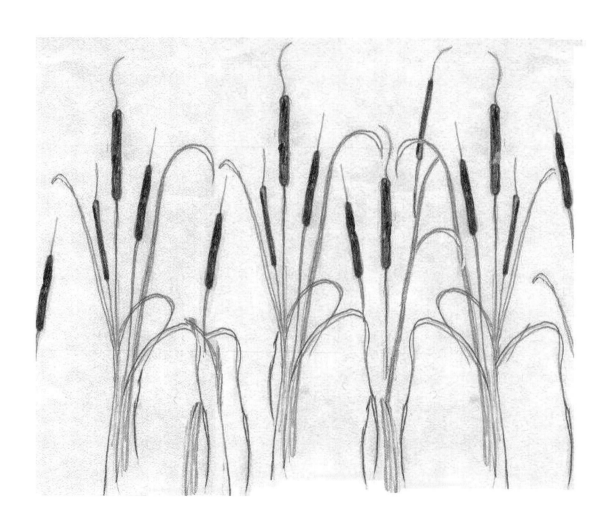

THE AUGUST SANCTUARY

      Tamarack Bay is the westernmost bay of Burntside Lake. High rocky cliffs and lowland bog make it a sanctuary for man and beast. Tamarack Creek flows into the lake here, feeding it from hundreds of springs, pools, run-off from beaver ponds, and spring snow melt.

      The west end of Burntside is dotted with many small islands. Some folks reside there for the summer. So does the wildlife.

      On an unnamed rock at the entrance to the bay, an osprey family took up residence in a dead pine tree one hundred feet tall. Since the late 1980's, they have faithfully returned each season to live out the call of the wild – namely by raising a family and teaching junior how to fly.

      If a boat or canoe cruises past, the adult birds begin a warning call which sounds like a series of fast repeated "peeps." But at night the high piercing call of a true member of the hawk family is recognizable as they hunt and fish.

      Loons find nesting grounds to their liking in the tall grass and rushes of the bog area surrounding the mouth of Tamarack Creek. They, too, are busy with one or two chicks for the summer. By the

end of August, the parent loons are demonstrating the way of life to their young. Seven different calls known to humans and countless survival techniques are lived out from early morning until the sun rises again. Their eerie calls echo down the lake, and in the August twilight they dance the age-old ritual of nodding and bowing to each other. In exuberance, they run and flap on the surface of the water, covering immeasurable ground in timeless moments, and glide to a stop with a "shush" of water beneath them.

Some wildlife resides "on the bay" all year long. The west end of Burntside houses some permanent residents on its southwest shore. Some are human; some not.

These residents reside permanently in the north country, enduring **the severe** and rejoicing in **the comfort**. Beaver, otter, mink, are among the swimmers that stay. Grouse, squirrels, rabbits, and deer reside in the forest. The human animal "settles in," too.

I sat on the dock step, naked except for the yellow towel around me, and drank in the view of August afterglow. The sun's rays showed peach across the tungsten-blue sky.

It was almost dark, but the rays shot miles into the sky from the western horizon.

This year, the end of August was hot. The cool air off the surface of the water met the warmer atmosphere, and a haze formed, making the tree-line on the opposite shore a bit difficult to discern. The smell of summer wind was still on the lake.

The loons began their evening serenade – the repertoire basically the same. I never tire of it.

Walking up the path from the lake, a slice of orange caught my eye. The August moon was appearing in full glory over the eastern birches – another repertoire of which I never tire. Slowly at first, then bounding into the night sky it lit the birch forest and made the entire woods glow.

I was aware of the sense of being enveloped in the womb of life, and savored the sacredness of the feeling. Anointed by the moment, a deep gratitude filled me. Ah, August. Ah, Summer. Ah, Jesus.

POPPLE GOLD

As night waned into early morning, the chill woke me and I sat up in my sleeping bag. Pulling the hood of the bag around my head and shoulders, I "scootched" to the door of the tent — a perfect place to wait for autumn sunrise. Stars were still reflected in the lake. Not a breath stirred.

It came, finally. First there was a light in the east, then a red glow on the white pine tree tops. Finally the sun cracked the horizon and emblazoned the already red and gold forest with morning fire.

Mist rose from the lake in such clouds that for a while it was difficult to know whether the day would be sunny or cloudy. At about eight a.m., the mist burned off, leaving the lake and gold-green forest shining in the sun.

Occasionally there is a day in Indian Summer that is forever etched on one's memory. This was one of those days. I hurried through a breakfast of oatmeal and tea. There wasn't a moment to lose. I planned to hike the Pow Wow Trail, part of which follows the Lake Three shoreline. My day pack was ready with the necessities for an all-day trek.

A short canoe paddle to the southeast corner of Lake Three wouldn't take much time. The lake was like glass, and the Grumman skimmed the surface quickly and silently. I appreciated the sense of being suspended in time.

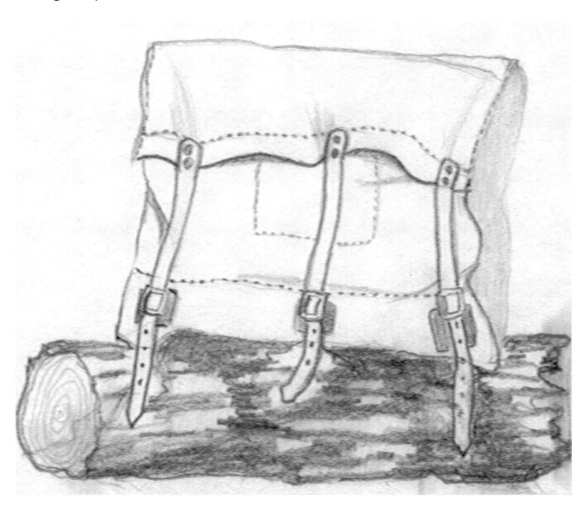

This was a day just past the peak of autumn color. Already the popple leaves were falling. A slight breeze made them whirly-gig to the forest floor. With a steady wind, only a third of the leaves would be left on the trees by tomorrow.

My attention was drawn to the balsams and Norway pine along the shoreline. Popple and birch leaves were caught in their needles, and made them look like decorated Christmas trees in the morning light.

A loon clothed in gray winter plumage, voiceless except for a hoarse attempt, swam past the canoe. Its mate joined him. Soon they would fly south, but for the time being they seemed unconcerned about future plans. They simply basked in the sunlight, water, and beauty of the moment.

The lake was a mirror which held in its reflection the gold and green of autumn past her peak. Very soon the reflection would be empty except for naked birches waiting for snow.

The hiking trail was ahead of me now, ensconced in gold and framed by a pale blue sky. Leaves lay like gold coins strewn on a brown carpet. Sunlight through the trees added to the shining aura.

I was glad that I had decided to spend the weekend canoeing and hiking. The woodpile and garden mulching were going to have to wait.

Silence pressed so loudly on my whole being that I paused to listen and reflect. A melody from Brahms' **Requiem** played into my consciousness. "How Lovely is Thy Dwelling Place, Oh Lord of Hosts." Appropriate, I thought. The forest prepares for winter. How did Brahms know?

    I landed on the rocky shore and lifted the canoe completely out of the water. It was time to hike. I checked my map and compass, shouldered my pack, and climbed the hilly path into popple gold.

TAMARACK WEATHER – TAMARACK GOLD

"It's the peak of the tamaracks," she said. "I'm glad we came." It was mid-October in BWCAW country. Winter change had come and gone. Now the real Indian Summer was making a visual and emotional impact as we paddled the canoe up the Tamarack Creek, which flows into the westernmost bay of Burntside Lake.

Privately, I refer to this particular piece of Burntside terrain as my sanctuary. Although it is an actual place, it is the mental image of this sanctuary that keeps me comforted in times of emotional stress or on-the-job anxiety. Today was just the sort of day to store in my memory bank for an as-yet-unknown day or time.

The sun was "in the grass." Otherwise nondescript marsh grass was glistening-dry. The tamaracks looked as though they were on fire. Their gold needles burned bright in the October sun.

There is a legend about this pine tree:

Of all the pines in the forest, this tree had the softest needles.

In the springtime, the tips of each branch bore a small flower which later became a small pine cone. It's wood was strong and firm, and the tree gave shelter to many birds and animals.

The tree prided itself on its beauty. It grew tall and strong near the edge of the water, and could see itself reflected in the water. It liked what it saw: a magnificent evergreen, a glory of the forest.

Eventually, summer waned into autumn and autumn into winter. The winds blew cold; the land froze still; the rhythm of winter was unrelenting and without mercy. Each creature of the forest set itself against icy blasts.

On a particular winter day, some birds paused and rested in the protective cover of the tamarack's thick green needles. "Oh tamarack tree," they chirped, "you re protection against the wind. Your needles are soft and cover us like a blanket. Could we please remain with you this winter in the shelter of your arms?"

The tamarack thought a moment and responded crisply, "I cannot give you shelter for the winter. In this cold, your coming and going would damage my needles. I would lose my beautiful image. I'm sorry, but you cannot stay."

Then, the Creator of the forest, who had heard the tamarack's response, spoke. "Because you have been selfish with the beauty and protective cover that I have given you, no longer will you have protection and beauty during wintertime." And to this day, the tamarack tree loses its needles in autumn and

unprotected bears the brunt of winter's chill.

The tree does "go out in a blaze of glory," however. It is the last tree to lose its "leaves" every fall. Tamarack gold isn't like popple gold. It comes later, when the woods are already naked, when birch and aspen have long since shed their raiment. Then and only then, when the deer are in winter dress and the Canadian geese are honking their way out of the northern marshes, do the tamarack begin to turn. Not many are there to view the final splendor. The human population, as well as the forest population, has turned its attentions to other things.

"It's the peak of the tamaracks," she said again. We munched pastrami sandwiches on the shore of Clark Lake, and I thought about tamarack trees. There they were, reflected in the unrippled, calm, dark water. The sky was a deep blue. Facing south into the fall sunshine, we were dry and warm. This was tamarack weather.

Upon returning to the cabin, I made a campfire. I planned to cook supper and enjoy the magic of flames and sparks. A gray jay flew to a feeding stump looking for a handout. There was nothing to be had, but he stayed there and smoothed his tuxedo with his beak.

I felt guilty enough to get up from my cooking to put out a few dry bread slices. The jay flew off with a warning call. He'll be back, I figured.

When I looked again, a blue jay had discovered the bread and looked as though it relished the cache. Another blue jay flew in but number one jay would have no part of sharing the bread. Flashes of blue in confrontation darting through a dead and gray-brown woods seemed almost florescent in the fall half-light.

Then in the autumn afterglow, the tamarack pines turned a crimson-gold and addressed us with a visual elegance. They stood like sentries in the lowlands at the entrance to the river.

At dusk I stood one more time to give my fire a stir. Autumn coolness got into my bones as I took a minute to lean on the rake handle. Then without warning a grouse burst from the undergrowth just ahead of me. That movement startled me. I settled down and watched the sparks glint in the twilight. Then, a second burst from the copse. A second grouse. There were two that the hunters didn't get.

Quiet enveloped me. I shuffled through the dry leaves and breathed deeply of this special moment. Tamarack weather encompassed the North.

FALL EVENING

The waning full moon came up orange over the trees in the northeast. A shiny yellow path rippled across the lake. It invited me to canoe its golden road.

At first it hung low in the sky. By midnight it had changed from yellow to white light and illuminated the white birch with yellow leaves just past their peak of autumn color. I reflected on the timeless feeling of change.

Late afternoon had found me at the public landing on the west end of Burntside Lake. It was crisp and I felt coolness from the water-cooled air on my flushed cheeks. I'd been hiking at a clip and had paused to rest and reflect at the lake's edge.

The roar of a truck motor startled me. I stepped to the brush at the side of the landing parking lot. A Department of Natural Resources (DNR) truck pulled up and stopped near the shore. A solitary driver jumped out. "Hi," he said. "Hi," I said.

"I've come to stock the lake with some walleye."

"Do you mind if I watch? I've never seen it done."

"Sure. But first I have to turn the truck around. The valves are on the wrong side."

With that he backed the truck around and to the water's edge. The truck was a 6-wheeler with a 175 gallon capacity fish tank in the box. He jumped out of the truck again and started rummaging in a plastic garbage can next to the fish tank. "Gotta put on boots," he said. He fished hip waders out of the garbage can and sat down on the grassy shoreline to change. Gortex boots came off. Thick sox in the boots were not used. He just slipped on the waders and started to open the valves of the tank.

"You out for a walk?"

"Yes. It's just beautiful, isn't it?"

"A great fall, although we could use a little more moisture."

"Um hum. But, there aren't many bugs."

He waded into the water and set out some plastic pipe. He emptied the walleye from the truck tank into the lake via a long corrugated plastic eight-inch hose which attached to the tank in a vacuum seal.

Then he was silent as the fish began to flow out of the tank and into the lake. Every once in a while, we saw a splash and a flip of the tail near the shoreline. A few remaining fish in the tank were removed via net and tossed gently into the shallows.

"These are nice walleye – quarter pounders," he said. "A good size to stock. I wish I had more. There are about forty pounds of fish here."

I looked at the fish. They were nice. "Some folks would call these keepers," he said.

"Yeah, but they're kind of small," said I, who would give my eye teeth for a limit walleye catch in season.

When he was done, he got out of the water. Gortex boots went back on. He stowed the waders in the garbage can and the garbage can in the truck box. The hose was wrapped and fit neatly into the far side of the box/tank area.

"So long," he said. The truck motor began to chug and he was off to his supper.

I walked up the landing road to 404. The woods were golden and the sun was pink-orange at sunset.

These are golden moments. A young white tail buck spooked out of a balsam copse. The silence of sunset time enfolded me as I hiked back to my supper.

CHANGE OF SEASON

I didn't see him at first. I was on an old logging trail in the Burntside State Forest. It was mid-October, and the world was yellow, just past its prime. I had stopped on the road to view the watery muskeg and to soak in the warmth of the autumn sun. Even at mid-day the shadows cast by the foliage were long and the tree line at the end of the swamp was dusky and dark brown. Wind rattled the dry birch leaves. Swamp grass rustled.

Then I heard it. A churning, mud-sucking commotion about 50 yards away and behind me. There he was in full autumn splendor – a black bull moose, in velvet, medium in size and sporting a good-sized rack. He seemed a bit puzzled as he looked around. I was upwind, but he must have caught my scent as I came into the bog area. He had been lunching on the moist, still green, plant life on the south-west corner of the bog.

It was some minutes before either of us moved. He stepped onto firmer ground, giving an unforgettable image of gleaming black body and antler against yellow-leafed background. I stood still, hoping for a closer look. After those priceless seconds, he moved

carefully into the balsam copse and disappeared.

The experience made my day. I was pleased and excited to be so fortunate. There are no guarantees on an afternoon hike in the woods – or anywhere else for that matter. Countless times, steps, and moments can come and go, and the hiker sees "the usual."

Two thoughts come to mind then. The first is that if a person goes into the woods often enough, odds are good that a special moment will overtake her. The second thought is this: "The usual" can turn into the unusual with a grateful attitude. It was enough to be out in 50 degree October sunshine. That was unusual and its own delight. The moose was a bonus.

As I approached the Clark Lake Road from the Tamarack River, another beauty assuaged my eyes. High atop the gray rocky river cliffs, burnished red splashed against the sky. It mixed with the blue-black river and golden tamaracks. My mind did a "double-take." Too late in the season for maples. These were pin oaks at their best – and lots of them.

It is a wondrous thing to behold autumn in her best dress. She's mature, aged by the spring and summer before her, and aware of the winter to come. The tears of summer rain have turned into the dancing of sunlight on this mellow season-wise land.

The memory of the color and gratitude for this experience will hold me through many winter nights.

The beaver house was right near the road. Funny about beavers. Don't they *know* that their choice of place lacks the large perspective? Or – is it I that lack the large perspective of being at one with nature?

Mid-afternoon brought a cloudiness to the walk. The wind picked up and I felt its sharpness in my left ear as I walked along the road. Rain wasn't in the forecast but by the time I reached the cabin, low and far away rolls of thunder sounded a prophecy.

The coffee pot was perking, and a mid-afternoon lunch of liver sausage, bread, cheese, and apple pie called me to the table. From the window, I heard the wind whine and saw the lake begin to "run."

Without any more warning, a cold hard rain began to pelt the porch. Yellow birch leaves swirled and fell like snow in the sudden squall. I watched in silence, knowing that this was the beginning of the end of autumn.

When the wind and rain finally stopped, the forest scene had changed. Tree leaves were two-thirds gone. I was aware of a starkness not present earlier in the autumn sunshine. The day continued to be gray. The wolf was around the corner. The lake reflected the dark sky.

It was time to embrace the season of black ice.

A paperback edition of *Reflections through Black Ice: Burntside speaks to her People* is available in northern Minnesota gift shops and stores so that you can take a copy with you as you canoe, bike, hike, fish, or spend time immersing body and spirit in natural beauty For prices and a listing of additional publications,
send an e-mail (cmoroni@spacestar.net)
or contact

Ely Chamber of Commerce
Ely, MN 55731

Send check or money order to
Singing River Publications
P.O. Box 72
Ely, MN 55731

Christine Moroni is a native of Ely, Minnesota. She has spent over twenty-five years teaching music in Minnesota public school classrooms with students ranging from kindergarten to community college. The natural beauty and constancy in the movement of the four seasons inspired this narrative. Since 1988, her articles on nature, music and spirituality have appeared in local, state and national publications.

She is also a composer of music and you can learn more about Christine by visiting her website: www.speravi.com/moroni

Helen Kuehlman, the visual artist has been resident of Ely, Minnesota for over thirty years. She has raised a family, taught school and now taps her own creative spirit through water color painting.